Ocelots

Victoria Blakemore

vblakemore.author@gmail.com

Copyright info/picture credits

Cover, Leonardo Mercon/Shutterstock; Page 3, Omariam/Shutterstock; Page 5, Karlos Lomsky/AdobeStock; Page 7, Omariam/Shutterstock; Page 9, rpbmedia/Adobestock; Pages 10-11, Cavan/AdobeStock; Page 13, henk Bogaard/AdobeStock; Page 15, Erni/AdobeStock; Page 17, ondrejprosicky/AdobeStock; Page 19, staoist520/AdobeStock; Page 21, slowmotiongli/AdobeStock; Page 23; PhotocechCZ/AdobeStock; Page 25, Lubos Chlubny/Shutterstock; Page 27, Danita Delimont/AdobeStock; Page 29, Andrea Poole/AdobeStock; Page 31, Omariam/AdobeStock; Page 33, Leonardo Mercon/Shutterstock

Table of Contents

What Are Ocelots?

Ocelots are mammals. They are members of the small cat family. Other small cats include margays, servals, and sand cats.

They have golden brown fur with white or cream bellies. They have patterns of black and brown spots and stripes.

Ocelot spots are **similar** to leopard spots. Many of them have brown in the middle of a black ring.

Size

Ocelots often grow to be between 28 and 40 inches long. This includes their tail, which is often between 10 and 16 inches long.

When they are fully grown, they can weigh between 15 and 35 pounds.

Male ocelots are larger than

female ocelots.

Physical Characteristics

Ocelots are known for the patterns of spots on their fur. No two ocelots have the same pattern. They are all **unique**. Their spots are different on both sides of their body.

Their eyes have a special layer that reflects light so they can see very well in the dark.

Like other cats, ocelots have

whiskers they use to sense what

is around them.

Habitat

The main habitat for ocelots is the rainforest. They like to be in places where it warm, with lots of plants.

Some ocelots have **adapted** to life in areas outside the rainforest. They can also be found in areas of scrubland.

Most ocelots are found in

South America.

Some small groups of ocelots can be found in parts of North America, including states like Texas and Arkansas.

Diet

Ocelots are **carnivores**. They

eat only meat.

Their diet is made up of small

animals such as frogs, birds,

iguanas, fish, and rodents.

They may also hunt for rabbits

and small deer.

Ocelots often hunt from above.

They watch their **prey** from the

treetops.

Ocelots are thought of as picky eaters. They remove the feathers and fur from their **prey** before eating.

They are known to take their **prey** up into the treetops to eat. This keeps them safe from larger **predators** on the ground. Their **predators** include jaguars and anacondas.

If an ocelot catches an animal
that is too large to eat at once,
it may cover it up and come
back later.

Communication

Ocelots use scent, sound, and movement to communicate with each other. They may arch their back if they sense danger.

Each ocelot has a **unique** scent. Male ocelots mark their **territory** with their scent. It tells other male ocelots to stay away.

Ocelots use sounds like chirps, soft meows, and growls. Loud yowls are used to find other ocelots.

17

Movement

Ocelots are very good at climbing. They need to be able to climb to avoid larger **predators** and hunt their own **prey**.

They are known to be good swimmers. Ocelots are sometimes seen swimming to catch fish or cross rivers.

Ocelot Kittens

Ocelots usually have a **litter** of one to two babies, or kittens. When they are born, kittens have their spots, but are more gray in color.

Their eyes are blue and change to brown after a few months.

The mother ocelot takes care of her kittens and keeps them safe in a den. She also teaches them how to hunt.

Ocelot Life

Ocelots are **nocturnal**. They are most active at night. They usually sleep in the bushes or treetops during the day.

Adult ocelots are **solitary**. They spend most of their time alone. Mothers and kittens usually stay together for one or two years.

In the wild, ocelots often live between seven and twelve years. They can live longer in **captivity**.

Ocelot or Margay?

Ocelots and margays are both small cats. They live in the same parts of the rainforest and look very **similar**.

They are so **similar** in coloring and spot patterns, that they can be very hard to tell apart.

Margays are smaller than

ocelots. They also have larger

eyes.

Population

The ocelots that are found in South America are not currently **endangered**.

There are more ocelots than any other kind of small cat in South America. However, their numbers are **declining**.

Only the kind of ocelot that

lives in America is **endangered**.

There are very few left.

Ocelots in Danger

The main threat ocelots are facing is the loss of their habitat. The areas where they live are being destroyed for materials, roads, and buildings.

When roads are built through habitats, animals are in danger of being hit by cars.

Ocelots used to be hunted just

for their fur. This isn't as

common now.

Helping Ocelots

While ocelots are not currently in trouble, there are ways that people are working to help them.

In some places, there are special wildlife **preserves** where animals like ocelots live. The animals that live here are safe from habitat loss.

In some countries, ocelots are protected by law. It is against the law to hunt them.

In parts of Texas, people are working to help ocelots. They are researching ways to help the small ocelot populations there to grow. They want the ocelots to have a better chance to **thrive** there.

Glossary

Adapted: changed, adjusted to

Captivity: animals that are kept by humans, not in the wild

Carnivore: an animal that eats only meat

Declining: getting smaller

Endangered: when an animal may become extinct

Litter: a group of animals that are born at the same time

Nocturnal: animals that are active and night

Predator: an animal that hunts other animals for food

Preserves: areas of land set up to protect plants and animals

Prey: animals that are hunted for food

Similar: having a likeness, resembling

Solitary: living alone

Territory: an area where an animal lives

Thrive: to do well, to grow and be healthy

Unique: different

About the Author

Victoria Blakemore is a first grade

teacher in Southwest Florida with a

passion for reading.

You can visit her at

www.enchantedinelementary.com

Also in This Series

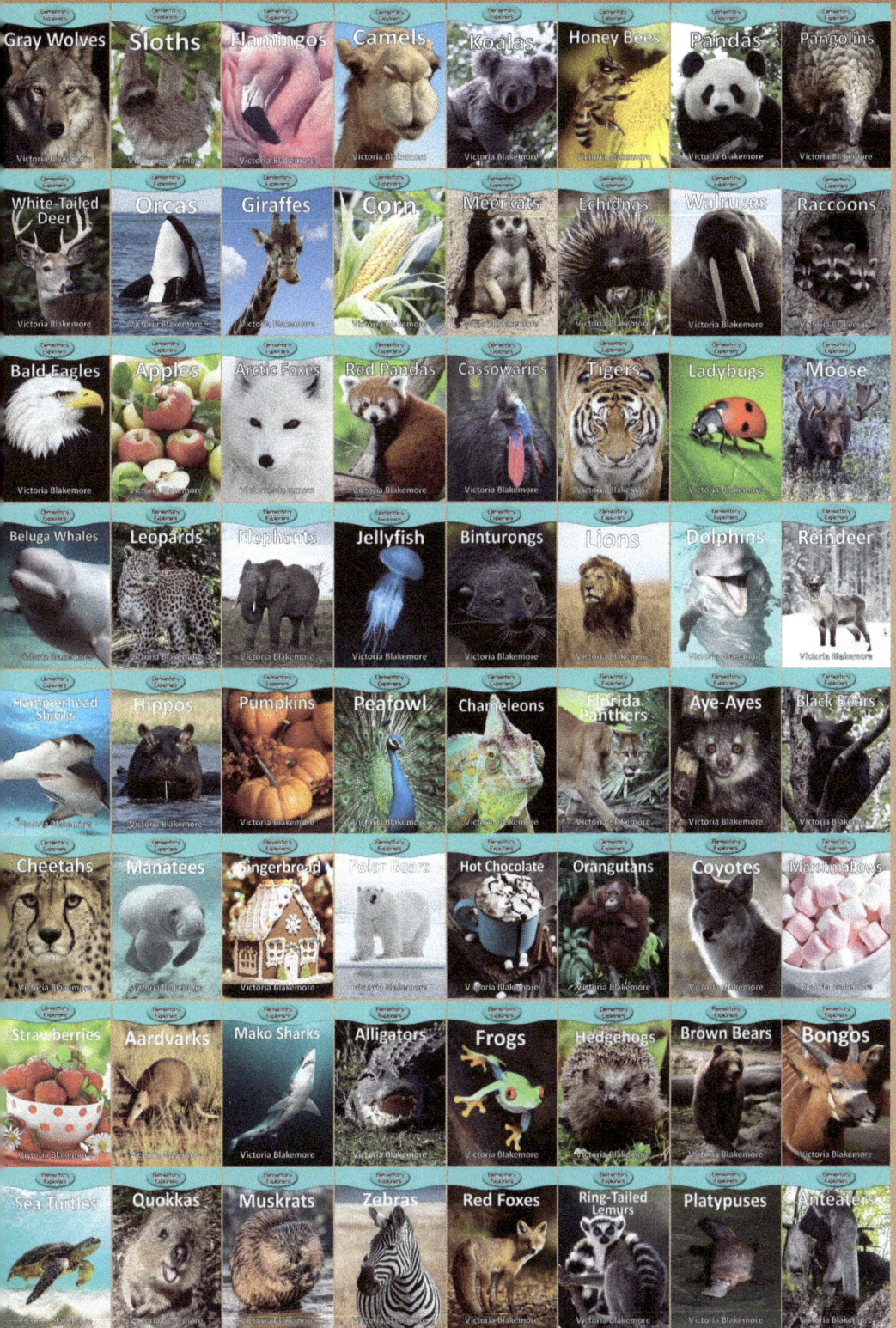

Also in This Series

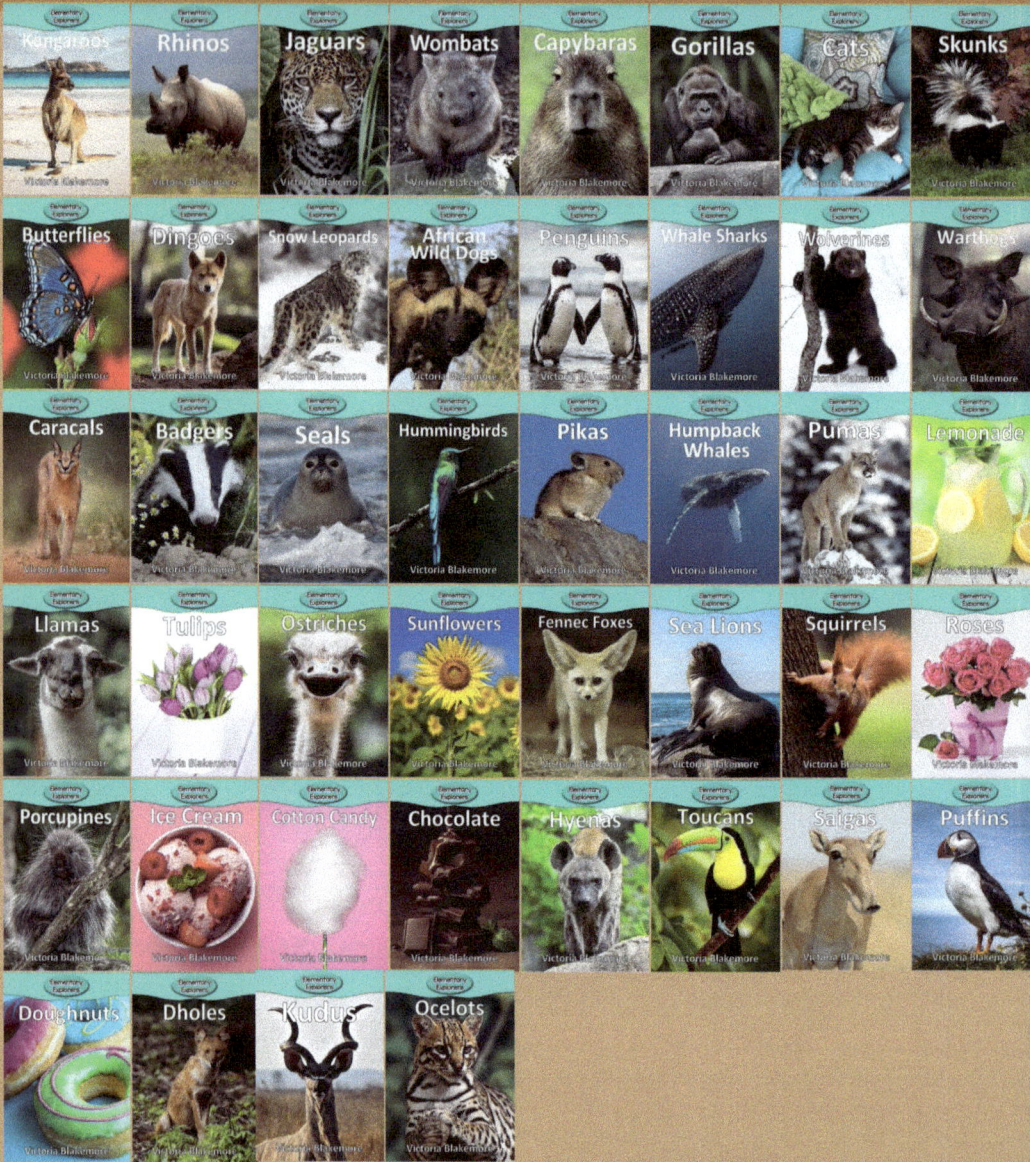

www.ingramcontent.com/pod-product-compliance
Lightning Source LLC
Chambersburg PA
CBHW052125030426
42335CB00025B/3112